WHEN BAD THINGS HAPPEN WHAT'S GOD'S PURPOSE

WILFRED BRIDGES SR.

ISBN: 978-1-969865-05-3 (sc)
ISBN: 978-1-969865-06-0 (e)

Rev. date: 09/24/2025

DEDICATION

For years I've often wondered why bad things happen to God-fearing Christians. When the doctor told my wife and **I** that she needed emergency surgery, we both were surprised and fearful. Our son was born premature, weighing one pound and thirteen ounces. As I saw him, I asked God "why?" No answer came, but I prayed and said, "God I don't believe you gave me my son just to take him back." I prayed and quoted Isaiah 53:5: "But he was wounded for our transgressions, he was bruised for our iniquities: the chastisement of our peace was upon him: and with his stripes we are healed."

Today my son is 25 years old, and doing very well, praise be to God. To Janice, who has been a loving wife for 37 years, thank you for pushing me to write my first book. I thank God for her spirit of tenacity and willingness to uplift our family before God. (My mother, Mrs. Ruth Bridges Summerall, what a blessing to have a mother who has overcome so much adversity. She overcame cancer this year with faith in God has been a joy to see. My mother has passed away, she lived a very good life, and we we're grateful to have her in our livesThe Lord God is truly worthy of all the praise, for it is He who called me to serve His people. I am simply amazed by His Grace.

CONTENTS

FOREWORD

I am honored to write this forward for my friend and brother, Pastor Bridges. He has met a need among believers in this excellent work, which answers an often-asked question today. Just as surely as good things happen to all, bad things happen to all as well, since God "sendeth rain on the just and on the unjust" (Matthew 5:45). When bad things happen, the believer usually asks God why but does not always look within for reason. These words encourage the believe to search and see if the bad is coming, not just arbitrarily from God, but because of their choices or disobedience, with an exhortation to "make it right" with God. Also, the section on suffering is encouraging as Pastor Bridges gives word of wisdom to endure in the spirit of Christ to receive God's favor. This book is a call to accountability for the believer, with the reminder that whether in good time or bad, it's all about God and not us.

Joseph Harris
Southeastern Baptist College

INTRODUCTION

"To every thing there is a season, and a time to every purpose under the heaven" (Ecclesiates 3:1). These are the words of King Solomon as he addressed the assembly. The theme of the verse is time. We all know that there is a time for many things, but when it comes to bad things, we often wonder if there's such a time, especially for a Christian. Being a believer of Jesus Christ, some bad things will come, but not so that it would overwhelm you. When there are consistencies of bad things that happen to you, you have to wonder why. You live according to God's words, you feel closer to Him, but why are bad things happening to you? Surely the Lord is our Shepherd; He watches over us and protects us from harm, seen or unseen, right! Is it wrong to think this way, feel this way, and to contemplate the matter? I don't think so. God is a mysterious God, meaning that He allows things to happen to make us aware that it's a never ending process of growing in His grace.

In a time of uncertainties, jobs lost, millions of people unemployed, health care that's not unaffordable, loss of homes, the wicked thriving, Christians leaving the faith, and the list goes on and on, it can cause you to ask, "Where is God?"

The psalmist said, "God is our refuge and strength, a very present help in trouble" (Psalm 46:1). God is right here, and that's a fact for those who believe His Word to be true. David was a man no different than us today. His Word to be true. David was a man no different than us today. He faced much opposition in troublesome times, came to a conclusion that God is always present, not just in the earth but everywhere. David asked where he shall go from God's spirit. How could he flee God's presence? David declared if he ascended up into heaven, God is there; if he went to hell, God is there; if he went to the uttermost part of the sea, God is there (Psalm 139:7-10). In other words, God is with us every single day and night. This certainly dispels the idea that God is not with us. He's everywhere at all times (omnipresence), His powers are unlimited (omnipotence), and He has all knowledge (omniscience).

A comforting response of a Christian should be, "Lord, you know me, you are with me, you created me, and your cause is my cause." Knowing God is with us still draws the question, why do bad things happen to those who follow Christ? And what is God's purpose?

As was stated by Solomon, there is a time for every purpose under the sun. Whatever God does, whatever

He allows, there is a purpose. God always talks to us in different ways or forms. Sometimes He reveals a sin that has gone unnoticed. He reminds us that we are His representatives, and He has a need for us to be humble (strength under control). God has not broken one promise that He has made, and we should keep the vows we made to Him. When bad things happen, use the bad things as an opportunity to serve Him. Have compassion and sympathy for the needs of others. Stop thinking in bondage, and stop procrastinating. Eliminate weakness by having faith in God to work out those difficult problems. As long as you are working for God, you are never a failure. You will experience some suffering, but when in doubt, you can always depend on God. The history of the Bible is God always pushing His people to move toward Him to receive the ultimate prize: heaven.

REVEALING OF SIN

I am a firm believer that sin, unforgiving or not asking for forgiveness, will cause considerable damage to your health and spiritual growth. God will always reveal sin to us, and once revealed He expects us to come to Him and ask for forgiveness. What God tells us to do , we should do without hesitation. To be forgiven of sin, God instructed us to ask-that is, to open the mouth and speak that sin out for forgiveness.

The Bible teaches that which goes in the mouth does not defiles the man, but that which comes out (Matthew 15:11). Jesus said, "From within, out if the heart of men, proceed evil thoughts, adulteries, fornications, murders, thefts, covetousness, wickedness, deceit, lasciviousness, an evil eye, blasphemy, pride, foolishness: Al these evil things come from within, and defile the man" (Mark 7:20-23). Sin is an issue that has to be dealth with, and there is no avoiding it. John said, "If we say that we have not sinned, we make him a liar, and his word is not in us" (1 John 2:10).

Throughout the Bible God had to reveal sin to His people in different ways because there different sins or ways of sinning. Take for example King David. He had the highest authority in the land and perhaps thought he could do whatever he wanted. Who would ever tell the king that he was wrong in the sight of God?

David committed a terrible sin by having an affair with Bathshedba. Her husband was at war, and she became pregnant with David's son. David called Uriah from the war to go to his wife. Uriah would not sleep with his wife because he felt guilt to be in the comfort of his wife while the other men were fighting. David commanded Uriah to be put on the front line, knowing he would be killed. David continued to be the godly king but had not confessed his sin to God. God used Nathan to reveal to David his sin with a parable. Nathan told David that there were two men; one was rich and the other poor. The rich man had many flocks of sheep, but the poor man had only one that was part of the family. A traveler came to the rich man, whom he prepared dinner for. Instead of the rich man taking one of his sheep, he took the poor man's sheep and prepared it for the rich traveler. After Nathan finished the story, David responded by saying, "Surely he must die." Nathan told David he was that man (2 Samuel 12:1-7).

David repented of his sin and realized that God revealed his sin to give him a second chance. **God has the power** to forgive, but that power is only activated when we confess to Him. The Apostle Paul said, "Let every soul be subject unto the higher powers. For there is no power but of God: the powers that are ordained of God (Romans 13:1). We are to honor authority especially when it is fair and just. David got forgiveness but his entire family suffered for his wrongful deeds. You may be carrying a sin that God has revealed. If so, ask God for forgiveness right now. If bad things are happening to you consistently, it could be a sin that has not been confessed to God for forgiveness.

Sin is deceitful; it can hide itself so well that you can forget what is and what's not sin. People can live a decent and moral life, but that's not a guarantee to heaven. A Christian must remember that proper worship is always in order. A constant diet of holiness keeps sin from penetrating the heart of the believer. We need the Word of God not only on our lips, but also most importantly in our hearts.

This was certainly true in the case of a rich young ruler. When Jesus was in Judea, many people surrounded Him to enquire about the law and His personal interpretation. A rich young man asked Jesus, "What good thing shall I do, that I may have eternal life?" Jesus replied, "Keep the commandments" (Matthew 19:16-17). The young man told Jesus that he had kept the commandments from his youth until Jesus told him to sell his possession and give it to the poor and follow him. The young man went away sad because he refused to give up his wealth for the glory of God. The sin that was revealed is that he loved his wealth more than the Lord. Please understand that when God directs your path, He's already made provision for all of your needs, it's a matter of faith and trust in Him. There are many who may say that they put God first, but on Sundays they have excuses. Do they give God what He commands like time, talent, and treasure? Do they make excuses of why they don't tithe? God instructs us to tithe; it's a commandment, not a choice. Jesus said "No man can serve two masters; for either he will hate the one, and love the other; or else he will hold on to the one, and despise the other. You cannot serve God and mammon [materials]" (Matthew 6:24). If there is something or someone that you honor more than God, ask the Lord God for forgiveness and put God first.

God is really merciful, and the test of time has proven it. He goes beyond the call of duty to bring us back into fellowship with Him. He uses different people, whether they are saved or unsaved, to encourage the believers to stand firm in His Word. The nonbeliever may not know that they are being used by God, but they certainly know when God is working.

When Abraham was traveling to the land that God promised, he encountered many enemies, but God defeated them all. There was one time that Abraham felt the need to lie about his relationship with his wife. As they were traveling through Egypt, Pharoah's soldier approached them. Abraham told his wife, Sarah, to lie and say she was is sister because he feared the King would have him killed if he knew Sarah was his wife. Pharaoh took Sarah, and Abraham's life was spared, but Pharaoh knew God was not pleased. God caused plagues to fall upon his kingdom. He brought Sarah back to Abraham and asked why he lied. He told Abraham to take his wife and leave. Then God revealed to Abraham that there was no need to fear and lie.

How many believers say they trust God no matter what, but when things seem certain to fail, they trust their logic more than God?

Psalm 34:8 says, "O taste and see that the Lord is good: blessed is the man that trusted in Him. "Trusting God does not mean you are going down some dark tunnel without light. Trusting God means He will lead you to the light while you are going through the tunnel. When you allow Him to lead you, you will see things you've never dreamed of seeing. Your heart will be filled with wondrous blessings that you cannot speak. God does these things not to impress us but to show us how much he loves us. (1 Corinthians 2:9).

When God reveals our sin, it is important to respond in proper time, because avoiding repenting could be deadly. It's sad to say, but God allows death to cause life to be birthed in others. Its sad that God had to go to the extreme of allowing death. When God commands us, we must obey-not part of the way, but all the way. Not fully obeying God leads to unexpected departure. This happened to a husband and wife who did the right thing but did not fully do as God instructed.

Ananias and Sapphira had sold some property and brought God his part but not the full amount. This was concerning tithes and how important it is to God. Once they were questioned about the amount, they lied to Peter. Peter told them it was not him that they lied to, but God. At that very moment, they both died-the husband first then his wife (Acts 5:1-11).

God does not judge every believer's sin with death, but in some situations He does (1 Corinthians 11:30; 1 John 5:16). Sin unto death is refusal to accept Christ as God's incarnated Son, habitual disobedience to God's commands, and consistent failure to love others. One of the greatest sins that Christians commit is not tithing. God's word is the law, and when we disobey, a crime is committed. God has instructed us of how much to give Him; a tenth (Genesis 28:22; Leviticus 27:32; Isaiah 6:13).

God instructed us when to give it; the first day of the week, Sunday (1 Corinthians 16:1-2). God has told us that when we tithe correctly, blessing will be given, but when we do not tithe, curses will be given (Malachi 3:6-11).

Many Christian are not tithing because of false teachers who say tithing is just the teaching of the Old Testament and it's not concerning the New Testament. These false teachers will be judged by God. Remember, Jesus honored all the Old Testament teachings concerning what should be given to God. Also remember that God has not changed, who are we to change God's Word simply because we don't want to give money.

I'm sure you know that there are more sins committed than just tithing. Whenever a person misses going to church, that's a sin according to Hebrews 10:25. Jesus Christ is the same yesterday, today, and forever (Hewbrews 13:8). When bad things happen to the Christians, could it be a sin that has not been repented of? God's purpose is for us to have a life of abundance according to His Word. God has revealed a sin you are doing, and you have not asked for forgiveness. If so, stop and ask Him to forgive you.

REPRESENTATIVE/ AMBASSADORS

The Bible says, "If a man be in Christ, he is a new creature: old things are passed away, behold all things are become new" (2 Corinthians 5:17). When the Lord Jesus is accepted as savior of a person's soul, that soul belongs to God. God authorized that soul to become an agent or delegate, meaning that soul has become part of God's body and is expected to cooperate fully with His plan. His plan involves living for Him, speaking for Him, working for Him, and loving for Him. When Christ was upon the earth, He was the representation of God. When you saw Him, you saw the face of God. He was the likeness or image of God. Now that we are Christian, we are like Christ. When people see us, they should see Christ.

Representative - Ones who is authorized as an agent or delegate; acting or having the power as an agent to serve as an example, specimen to set forth a likeness or image of. Ambassador - An accredited diplomatic agent of the highest rank, appointed as the representative serving as a person of good will.

As a representative of Christ, people become a symbol of righteousness. This is recognized in their living (mannerism), speech, and action. To have such attributes, God must dwell within a person's heart, soul, mind, and spirit. This allows a person to become an ambassador. The Apostle Paul represented Christ and encouraged the believers to become ambassadors. Sin separates us from God, and through Christ we are reconciled back to God. Paul said, "Now then we are ambassadors for Christ as though God did beseech you by us: we pray you in Christ's stead, be ye reconciled to God" (2 Corinthians 5:20).

How do you think God feels when we misrepresent Him? Misrepresentation is a sin in the sight of God. Whenever a child disrespects his parents, he has broken God's commandments. We are God's children and if we disrespect Him, we have sinned. Galatians 6:7 says, "Be not deceived for God is not mocked, whatsoever man sows that shall he also reap."

When a country needs someone to represent, they send an individual who is born a citizen of that country. They send someone who is going to be committed to the fundamental teaching of that country. That means this person believes in those fundamentals and will uphold them no matter who is against them. This representation took place in the teaching of that country, receiving fully in the mind and heart of a person to become an ambassador. So it should be with a Christian when he becomes one in Christ. It is vital that a new believer receives the fundamental teaching of Jesus Christ. Whenever a Christian is inconsistent in his living for Christ, the foundation has not fully been received or given because of lack of teaching. To represent Christ, the fundamental teaching of repentance (2 Corinthians 7:10), forgiveness (Ephesians 1:6-7), confession of sin (Romans 10:9), believing (John 3:16), and faith (Hebrews 11:1,6) must be properly taught with clarity.

You cannot become a representative and an ambassador of Christ if you don't have the fundamental teaching of salvation. Let's apply wisdom to fundamentals. Understanding is knowledge that transforms into power. Power is a source that allows you to do and gives you the ability to get. Wisdom is now applied as experience that makes a person a reliable source.

For one of the wisest men in the Bible, Solomon, perception of wisdom is to be possessed with the teaching of God. He expresses how important it is to be influenced quickly by the Word of God. Do not delay or put off getting the understanding of who God is and what His purpose is for you. Solomon said, "The Lord possessed me in the beginning of his way, before his works of old" (Proverbs 8:22).

To move from representative to ambassador, the Word (logos) teaches us from faith to faith the truth about ourselves. Faith in trusting God comes by doing His Word. James said, "Whoso looks into the perfect law of liberty, and continue therein, he being not a forgetful hearer, but a doer of the work, this man shall be blessed in his deed" (James 1:25). The Word illuminates darkness and causes a deeper effect on the believer's heart. No longer is the Word of God in the mind but most importantly sealed in the heart. The believer does not need approval of men, money to work for Christ, or someone to be with them to serve and worship Christ. His heart is filled with the love of God through Jesus. The Bible says, "Love work no ill to his neighbor: therefore love is the fulfilling of the law" (Romans 13:10; 2 Corinthians 5:14; John 5:42).

Many Christians are representatives but not ambassadors because they are still in love or consumed with the blessings of God rather than God. This is why we have two types of Christians: carnal and spiritual. Carnality is a Christian that believes in God but does not trust Him fully. A spiritual Christian trusts God no matter what the circumstances are. Solomon said, "Hear instruction, and be wise, and refuse it not. Blessed is the man that hears me, watching daily at my gates, waiting at the post of my doors. For whoso find me finds lie, and shall obtain favor of the Lord" (Proverbs 8:33-35).

When bad things happen, what's God purpose? We have a lot of representatives but few ambassadors. Is it a sin not to represent Christ? Is it a sin not represent Christ? Yes! Jesus said if you are ashamed to own Him (represent) before men, then likewise He would be a shame to own you before God and his holy angels (Mark 8:38). When a Christian hears a conversation of whether or not God is real, what is he to say? When someone says Jesus is not the Son of God but a great prophet of God, what does a Christian do? If you know that you have been redeemed, you'll defend God at all costs.

When God's commandments are broken, the ambassador is

demoted and reprimanded for his mistakes. God does not understand sin, but He's so merciful that He's given us something called forgiveness, grace, and mercy. An ambassador doesn't have to lose his position or leave because of his mistakes. If one continues in habitual sins and thinks he is okay, he becomes a bad representative. You cannot honor God and not honor His word. If a person says, "I love my parents," but do not do what his parents ask him to do, he becomes a hypocrite. People today are representing position, but their hearts are not of an ambassador. They have the name of the position, but not the works that are required-hypocrite. Jesus put it this way: "People draw near unto me with their mouth and honor me with their lips, but their heart is far from me" (Matthew 15:8). To represent Christ is an honor, and to be His ambassador is commitment and loyalty.

I was watching Dateline one night about a man who was murdered by his ex-girlfriend. Upon waiting on the trail to take place, the ex-girlfriend was granted bail and was staying with her oldest son. The parents of the deceased man knew the ex-girlfriend killed their son. They later found out that the ex-girlfriend was pregnant with their son's baby. The parents of the murdered man were granted visitation rights to see their new grandson. The grandparents would not do anything to upset the ex-girlfriend because they knew once in a court, the ex-girlfriend would be found guilty. The little boy liked his grandparents more than his biological mother. The mother of the murdered man said that the ex-girlfriend would get so mad and furious when the baby boy wanted his grandparents. She said at those moments, she saw what her son saw before he died.

One day, the ex-girlfriend took her baby and tied him around her and jumped into the ocean and drowned herself and the baby. The grandparents were devastated, and their remarks were those of great ambassadors. The grandmother said, " I had a great childhood, wonderful parents that loved me, and a great career. I have a husband that I love and a son that I cherished, and God has always been there. I am in a pit now, and God is with us."

Today their faith in God has rewritten the child protection laws concerning courts releasing children into the care of parents suspected of committing crimes. When things were good, they were representatives, but when bad things happened, they became ambassadors. They are now helping thousands of children like their grandson and said they will continue to do so. Don't just talk the talk, but also walk the walk. When bad things happen, what's God purpose? Representatives show the way, ambassadors live the way.

HUMBLENESS

Humble- modest in spirit; not proud, unpretentious: deeply or courteously respectful.

When I think of humbleness, I think about Jesus above all others. To think of the power that He possessed and what He did with that power and yet humbled himself to die on a cross, He was truly humble. In Philippians 2:5-8, Paul taught on the humbleness of Jesus when he said, "Let this mind be in you, which was also in Christ Jesus. Who, being in the form of God, thought it not robbery to be equal with God. But made himself of no reputation, and took upon Him the form of a servant, and was made in the likeness of men. And being found in fashion as a man, he humbled himself, and became obedient unto death, even the death of the cross."

Those scriptures are talking about the Son of God, who could have acted with full authority of His deity, but He did not.

Can you imagine being God in the flesh and having a radical crowd ready to kill you for being innocent? With just a wave of His hand, all could have died, but Jesus was so in control. He allowed them to live. Why? To show that His mercy goes even to the worst type of people. How many times should we have been judged harshly, but Jesus forgave us just because He loves us? How many times should we have experienced the full wrath of God, but He gave us another chance without punishment? Do you have the temperament of Jesus? When bad things happen, what's God purpose?

As we all know, disobeying God brings dangerous consequences. One of the major problems with Christians today is pride. It is manifested in conversation, witnessing, fellowshipping, and activities concerning Christ in giving of time, talent, and treasure. I was looking at the Christians Network one day and Joyce Meyers was talking about how Christians are so rude when conferences are held at various hotels. She asks that no one be rude at breakfast, lunch, and dinner. She asks for all Christians to be humble even if they don't get the service they think they are supposed to get. Say, "Thank you," Yes, sir," and "No, sir." Be an example of Christ. I agree with her. Christians are to be leaders for Christ, not the devil. How many people are turned away from Christ because of rude Chrisitans?

When God call us to do His will, we should do it in a modest spirit, not pretentious, as if we are better than others. Samson, who was endowed with great strength, was very pretentious. God used him to defeat the Philistines, but he fell far short of God's standard with his sin and disobedience. He was a Nazarite and the last of the judges or military leaders. His life is a clear warning against the dangers of self-indulgency and lack of discipline. In spite of his heroic physical deeds of killing a young lion, killing a thousand Philistines with the jawbone of a donkey, and carrying away the massive gate of Gaza, he nevertheless violated all three aspects of the Nazarite vow. He ate honey from a dead lion, attended a drinking feast, and had his hair cut (Judges 13:4,5). Although he did God's will, it was done with little humbleness. The Bible says, "Humble yourselves therefore under the mighty hand of God, that He may exalt you in due time. Casting all your care upon Him; for He cares for you." Be sober, be vigilant; because your adversary the devil, as a roaring lion, walketh about seeking whom he may devour (1 Peter 5:6-8). Humbleness will keep you watching with a warrior mentality. When humbleness is lost, then anger, malice, hate, and other evil spirits will consume the heart.

Being humble has its benefits. Another definition of humbleness is meekness. Jesus rewards those who humble themselves to His command. Take the scripture that says, "Blessed are the meek for they shall inherit the earth"

(Matthew 5:5). This means that those who have been humbled before God will not only inherit the blessing of heaven, but will also ultimately share in the kingdom of God on earth.

Humbleness is part of seed time and harvest. Who can deny the fact that all things in the earth will not give you security and peace? So humbleness unto God will grant peace in the earth and peace in heaven. In Psalm 37:11, it says, "But the meek shall inherit the earth; and shall delight themselves in the abundance of peace." We must believe in the Bible and take it as God's Word; this requires absolute faith. No question, no debate, just a trust that God's Word is true. We know the Lord's commandments; keeping the law from an outward perceptive is good, but it's no good if you don't believe in the heart. There are laws that we keep in the natural world, and we do not like them. Who likes to be taxed for working? No one, but we pay them. For decades this law has been placed on all who work. We don't like it, but we honor it. A humble Christian will always put God above anybody or anything. We cannot just do what God says from an outward perspective, but inwardly we must obey, This requires faith, honor, and love.

Paul put it best when he said, "For the promise, that he should be the heir of the world, was not to Abraham, or to his seed, through the law, but through the righteousness of faith (Romans 4:13).

Humbleness is a virtue of Christ and causes great things to manifest through us in the earth. Martin Luther King, Jr. exemplified humbleness by leading a non-violent campaign to acquire equal rights for all human beings. It was his humbleness of the teaching of Jesus that made him an effective witness. A lot of bad things happened to him, but he remained faithful to the cause of peace. God is the God of peace, but He is also the God of wrath. He expects us to be the humble servants so that peace can be established in the earth. Now we can understand that humbleness creates peace. Peace does not create humbleness. This humbleness that Jesus displayed can only be achieved in a believer by having the mind of Christ.

Jesus made no reputation of himself, but His humbleness caused a reputation. The phrase "made he of no reputation" comes from the Greek word kenosis, for emptying (Phillipians 2:7). He voluntarily submitted Himself to the will of the Father. We must have this same trust, devotion, honor, and love of Christ to empty ourselves to God.

One of the most humbling stories can be found in the Bible is the book of Ruth. Ruth left everything she had and followed and looked after her aging mother-in-law, Naomi. Her husband had died, and her sisters-in-law were gone back to their native land. She followed Naomi into unknown territory, stayed wherever Naomi stayed, abandoned her people for Naomi's people, accepted God, and died where Naomi died (Ruth 1:16-17). Ruth was wise because she knew God was with Naomi. The Bible says, "Surely he scorneth the scorners: but he giveth grace unto the lowly. The wise shall inherit glory: but shame shall be the promotion of fools" (Proverbs 3:34-35). Ruth's humbleness brought her marriage to Naomi's cousin, Boaz, who was rich. A bad thing happened to Naomi and Ruth, but God's purpose was fulfilled. Between the marriage of Ruth and Boaz, Obed was born. Obed is the father of Jessie, Jessie is the father of David, and Jesus is from the lineage of David. Humbleness will always produce great greatness.

In the case of Samson, he caused much harm to himself because he was not humble before God. But once he was captured, he humbled himself before God and was exalted by killing thousands of Philistines as a hero of faith. The faith came when he realized that the bad things happened because he would not humble himself to God's purpose. Humbleness does four things:

Glorifies God
Defeats Satan
Creates Peace
Achieves Greatness

Whosoever therefore shall humble himself as this little child, the same is greatest in the kingdom of heaven.

— Matthew 18

VOW KEEPER

Vow- To make a solemn promise, a pledge of faithfulness to do, and to swear.

How many vows we as Christians have made and broken without any remorse? To God it must seem mundane for His people not to keep their vows. My purpose in writing this book is to prove that when bad things happen, it's not so much the devil that causes bad things to happen to us, but we cause bad things to happen to ourselves. God's wrath can be upon a believer simply because a vow has been broken. This can cause a lifetime of aggravating trials that can be avoided if the vows made to God are kept. Just read about Solomon who was the preacher and the king. Solomon gave warnings of speaking too fast to God about what you will and will not do. As a matter of fact, Solomon says that you should say very few words to God. In other words, be quiet and listen to God. What possibly can you inform God about that He does not already know? Solomon put it this way: " When thou vowest a vow unto God, defer not to pay it; for he hath no pleasure in fools: pay that which thou hast vowed. Better is it that thou shouldest not vow, than that thou shouldest vow and not pay. Suffer not thy mouth to cause thy flesh to sin; neither say thou before the angel, that it was an error: wherefore should God be angry at thy voice, and destroy the work of thine hands? For in the multitude of dreams and many words there are also divers vanities: but fear thou God" (Ecclesiastes 5:4-8).

Solomon was the wisest man alive and could tell us a thing or two about vows and how they would affect those who break them.

Solomon broke his vow with God when he married foreign wives and allowed them to worship idol gods. God was so displeased that he laid Solomon to rest beside his father David.

Every vow that God made He has done. God will not break His promises of what He will do or what he will not do. Whatever you speak, it is you, and your conversations should be of life and not death. Jesus taught that no one should swear by any means, person, or thing. We have to be careful in our conversation, because "the power of life and death is in the tongue, and those who love it shall eat the fruit thereof" (Proverbs 18:21). Whenever you became a Christian, you made a pledge of faithfulness unto the teaching of Jesus Christ. When we were in sin, we were the living dead. Once Jesus saved our souls, we were alive in Jesus Christ. To maintain our spiritual growth in the grace of the Lord, a Christian must partake of God's Word daily.

You have to maintain a steady diet of reading and studying the Word so life can be produced with every breath.

The Bible says in 2 Peter 3:9, "The Lord is not slack concerning his promise, as some men count slackness; but is longsuffering to usward, not willing that any should perish, but that all should come to repentance." Just think, whenever a vow is paid to God, what kind of life will you have? Can you imagine how blessed you will become? A lot of bad things happen to the believer because he has actions of selfishness; pride; conceit; jealousy; belittling others' ideas; negative responses; thinking more highly than he should; lying; backbiting; glorying in people's failures; being a poor follower of the husband; being disrespectful to his wife, the pastor, the supervisor; or never giving God time, talent, and treasures. How in the world does one think goodness is going to follow him a week or a day? Believe me, there are people today who have bad things happening to them every day. Brothers and sisters, that's not God intention for His children. You cannot please God from an outward perceptive. Having the praise of men is vanity, having the praise of God is assurance, assurance that keeping your vows is going to heal you from all diseases, prosper your work, establish your fellowship, and increase your faith.

Hebrews 11:6: But without faith it is impossible to please Him: for he that cometh to God must believe that He is, and that He is a rewarder of them that diligently seek Him.

The word diligently is an action word. It takes effort to keep your vows; it takes persistent effort to receive your rewards from God.

God is very serious about vows, just read the church covenant and ask yourself how serious are you? God is so serious about His Word that He will let His wrath fall on those who violate it. When God instructed Moses to ordain Aaron and his sons as the priests of Israel, he gave every person a role to perform. Two sons of Aaron, Nadab and Abihu, were responsible for lighting the fire or coal in the tabernacle for the incense. They used what the Bible calls "strange fire," which the Lord commanded them not to do. The Lord was not pleased at all. The Bible says, " And there went out fire from the Lord, and devoured them, and they die before the Lord" (Leviticus 10:2)

Do you think God wasn't serious about vows? Theologians said that it was at the wrong time, the coals were not taken from the altar, and perhaps they were drunk, which seems more likely because of verse 9. Nevertheless, God's Word is law, and it will not return back void.

Deuteronomy 23:21 says, "When thou shalt vow a vow unto the Lord thy God, thou shalt not slack to pay it: for the Lord thy God will surely require it of thee; and it would be sin in thee." Whenever sin abides, bad things will happen to those who will not repent, not only with their mouth but also with actions.

Take for example Zacchaeus, a publican described as a "chief tax collector" who was rich. He wanted to see Jesus for himself so he climbed a tree. Once Jesus saw him, He told him to come down, for he must abide at his house. Zacchaeus was so thrilled that he began to confess his sin and to pay God his vow. Zacchaeus said, "Behold, Lord, the half of my goods I have to the poor: and if I have taken anything from any man by false accusations, I restore him fourfold. Jesus said, This day salvation come to this house, for as much as he also is a son of Abraham" (Luke 19:8-10).

Zacchaeus knew what his real problem was. He **had** many enemies, had sleepless nights, was hated by his own people, had no true friends, and had a soul that was in turmoil. Once he paid his vow to the Lord, his bad days turned into good days.

Once you've paid your vow to God, expect all things to work together for good to you who loves God, **for you are called** accordingly to His purpose Romans 8:28). I do believe that an enemy can last for a very long time if you don't keep your vow unto the Lord. Breaking a vow is putting a curse upon you. Don't let the enemy have power over your blessings. When bad things happen, God's purpose is to deliver you from those bad things. Remember, the enemy comes to steal, kill, and destroy (John 10:10). Keep your vow; and God will take care of your enemies. God, who embodies a burning zeal for righteousness and justice, quickly arises to the defense of His own. The prophet Nahum pictured God standing on the mountain pouring out wrath upon the enemies of those who kept their vows. And he says, "Behold upon the mountains the feet of him that bringeth good tidings, that publisheth peace! O Judah, keep thy solemn feasts, perform thy vows:, for the wicked shall no more pass through thee; he is utterly cut off (Nahum 1:15).

REALIZE YOUR WORTH

There is a great cost that has been given for this world and the primary existence of life as we know it. That cost is the precious blood of Jesus Christ. One reason Jesus willingly died for our sins was because he knew his "worth" to God and us. I assure you that not one dop of blood was wasted when Christ bled on the cross. Those who argue the fact that Christ did not die for everyone is blinded by Satan. Those who have accepted Christ can testify how His blood took away their sins: murder, theft, prostitution, worshipping idol gods, adultery, fornication, pornography, drug addiction, spousal abuse, mocking, child abuse, and atheism, just to mention a few. They would gladly tell anyone that Christ's dying was not in vain. You cannot put a price on the cleaning and washing away of sins. All the silver and gold in this world cannot buy such a precious gift.

Often God has to remind us of what affords us the opportunity for such a life that we live. Whether it's through pastors, evangelists, teachers, and bishops, God never lets us forget what bought our freedom. The Bible declares in 1 Corinthians 6:19-20: "What Know ye not that your body is the temple of the Holy Ghost which is in you, which ye have of God, and ye are not your own? For ye are bought with a price: therefore glorify God in your body, and in your spirit, which are God's "

God has very good reason to have ownership of human beings because: (1) God made us; and (2) He purchased us by His Son's blood. Every human being has freedom of choice. For all of us who choose to follow Chrit, His blood has profound significance.

How profound is it for the believer? First Peter 2:9 says, "But ye are a chosen generation, a royal priesthood, a holy nation, a peculiar people; that ye should show forth the praises of him who hath called you out of darkness into his marvelous light." This is very profound and significant for those who are called by God. Whenever God calls you out to do his will, it's serious business. Whenever we neglect God, He has no choice but to stand back, because He gave us freedom of choice. God won't force Himself on anyone, but when we refuse to do His will, bad things will happen.

When Israel was to be a holy nation but refused to do so , she was in exile for many years. For generations to holy nation was at the foot of her enemies. The priesthood was not royal priests because of impropriety. The people who once were special (preculiar) in God's eye were no longer special. Once you are not special in his eyes, how special can you be to others? God gave his Son not only to buy our Soul from sin, but that we show gratitude and honor for His amazing grace. The blessed fact that our body is the temple of the Holy Spirit should indicate what we are worth to God. All believers must show their worth.

God needs us to be a living example not only to the sinners, but to the believers as well. Paul said that we need to be examples in several ways: (1) in word (living), (2) in conversation, (3) in charity (love), (4) in spirit, (5) in faith, and (6) in purity (1 Timothy 4:12). Notice Paul uses the world in to indicate that the believe should posses these spiritual qualities within their inner being. All these gifts will cause the believer to prosper. God not only created us in His image, but also created us to prosper for Him. This means that the process of growing and being worthy as a created being in the image of God starts within ourselves. God has given all the necessary equipment to the believers to be worthy of His call. A healthy inside produces a healthy outside.

The Apostle John put it this way: Beloved, I wish above all things that thou mayest prosper and be in health, even as the soul prospereth (3 John 2). When your soul prospers, the body will be good health as well. Moses followed the voices of God. Everything God told him to do, he did. Nothing could stop Moses, because he carried out the Word of God. There is no force on earth or in earth that can stop the power of God. When He speaks, it will come

To pass. The people who carry out God's Word are worth more than all the silver and gold in the world.

What about those who have God's World but will not do anything with the Word? Good things will not come to those who know God's Word and refused to perform it. There is a truth to "if you don't use what you got, you will loose it." It's a bad thing when God takes your gifts. When this happens, a believer must look within themselves to make a transformation. If the believer does not change, they can expect a life of confusion, animosity, disportion, calamity, blindness, and hypocrisy. Matthew 5:13 says, "Ye are the salt of the earth: but if the salts have lost his savor, wherewith shall it be salted? It is to be cast out, and to be trodden under foot of men." Are you helping the world or helping yourself to the world? Do you know your worth to society? God certainly does because He have you what you got. As salt, every believer should know that salt does. Salt does four primary things: (1) add flavoring, (2) acts as a preservative, (3) melts coldness, and (4) heals wounds. Every Christian should ask themselves if they are adding to life or taking away from it. Do you enlighten or cause confusion? Do you preserve the fellowship of other Christians? Do you bring a joy to others? Are you a talker an not a doer? Can you inspire, motivate, encourage, and forgive? The Pharisees were supposed to be a salt to the people, but they were heavy taskmasters. When people **left** their present, they were worse off and dreaded to come back to the temple.

The expression on their faces was not of peace but that of terrible things to come. The Pharisees were burdened givers rather than burdened helpers. It's a terrible thing when a Christian becomes the sword for the enemy and not the sword for the Lord.

God will allow bad things to happen for those who lose site of their worth. Please understand that the blood of Jesus cannot be wasted. Any hindrance of God's plan will be dealt with, and that can cause a lot of trouble. Jonah refused to tell the people of Nineveh the danger of disobeying God, and bad things happened to him. He stayed in the darkness for the nights in a whale's belly. Jacob stole his brother's birthright, and spent fourteen years in fear laboring for his uncle. How many people leave the church because of pride and not respect authority that God has given? When God has given you a ministry in a particular church, fulfill it until God directs you to another place. Its dangerous to say God directed you to move when He has not. Jesus said, "And in the same house remain, eating and drinking such things as they give: for the laborer is worthy of his hire. Go not from house to house" (Luke 10:7). This is significant for those who are getting the proper food, drinking from the cup of the Lord, and growing from the ministry.

When you receive the truth, don't run because it hurts; stay and get healed. Running from church to church and preacher is not going to solve anything. If Jesus tells us not to do it, then we shouldn't do it. If we do the

Opposite, bad things will happen. God has placed a value in you to fulfill his purpose at a particular place and time. Going to another house and not completing the mission in the first house only cause problems in the "Body of Christ." Realize your worth right where you are.

OPPORTUNITY

Life sometimes can teach us a hard lesson if we let it. When things turn from bad to worse, it's hard to understand what God's purpose is. One should hope for things to get better, but hope has it limitations even when it's in Jesus Christ. Hope has no substance; it has a goal. We as Christians hope to see Jesus soon; our hope, our goal is to be with Him soon. Faith in Christ make our hope, our goal, a reality. This is why we believe, even when hope is fading away and situations seems to be turning for the worse and there is no possible way of it getting better. Faith in Christ establishes a trust in our heart that He makes the impossible possible. Every bad situation has the potential of produce an opportunity for Christian growth and benefits.

Opportunity - favorable occasion

The Apostle Paul was one that could a bad situation and use it to gain victory for the Lord. Paul was in bondage most of his life, but when you read his epistles, you wouldn't think so. Paul, on one occasions, was sailing to Rome to stand trial before Caesar. This was on his third missionary journey. While sailing on the sea, a strong wind came against the ship. The ship was tossed so that they had to lighten it by throwing off certain supplies. The storm grew worse and worse until it was life threatening. The Bible described it this way: "And when neither sun nor stars in many days appeared, and no small tempest lay on us, all hope that we should be saved was taken away " (Acts 27:20).

Now, what you just read is a really bad situation. Paul was a prisoner on a ship taking him to be on trial, and then a terrible storm drove the ship wherever it liked. Most of us would **wonder** what he had done to cause such despair. Well, it was not all about Paul but everything about God. God's purpose is always getting us to have confidence in Him no matter what **calamities we are facing.** The bible tells us, "Trust in the Lord, and do good; so shalt thou dwell in the land, and verily thou shalt be fed. Delight thyself also in the Lord; and he shall give thee the desires of thine heart. Commit thy way unto the Lord; trust also in him; and he shall bring it to pass (Psalm 37:3-5).

How often has a unfavorable occasion happened to us and we failed to trust in God? Those moments of opportunities to glorify Him are vital for the sinners and Christians growth. God wanted us to take our eyes off the terrible storms and trust in Him to be greater than any storm. When Peter asked Jesus to let him come on the water. Jesus said, "Come." Peter walked on water, but he looked at the terrible waves and lost focus on Jesus. He began to sink and in desperation called on Jesus. Jesus rescued him. Jesus said to Peter, "O thou of little faith, why did thou doubt?" (Matthew 14:31). It's a divine fact, that when bad things happen, God's plan is to try our faith so that it will come forth as pure gold. It **displeases** God when we doubt Him. He's not a liar, does not know how to lie, and has never lied. Second Peter 3:9 says, "The Lord is not slack concerning His promise, as some men counts slackness; but is long-suffering to us ward, not willing that any should perish, but that all should come to repentance" How many times have we failed to glorify and trust God when it looked like certain doom? We need to repent and as God for faith to believe no matter what our eyes see.

When the Apostle Paul was on the ship that was sinking (Acts 27:18), the crew began to lighten the ship. They cast off lesser valuables, hoping this would help the ship remain afloat. It is important also for Christians to get rid of the things we don't need in our lives, such as overreacting, smoking, drinking, procrastinating, negative thinking, jealousy, doubting, lust, inconsistency, blaming others, lack of studying the Word, praying because of need and not out of love, wrong atmosphere, and people. The Bible teaches us to "come from among the world, and be separate, and not to touch the unclean thing; God would receive you and be a father to you" (2 Corinthians 6:17-18). There are proven cases in which bad things happen when we disobey God.

God goes to the extent with his children. He allows for bad things to happen because it's the only way to get some peoples attention. It is in that moment that you realize how far you are from God. Some people don't get that they are in a bad situation until it's too late. God always gives chances of representative and forgiveness. When Paul and the other men were in the storm for the third day, they saw no sun, moon, or stars; all hope of being saved was taken away (Acts 27:20). God has every person's attention because they recognized a bad situation. Every believer has a opportunity to bring to God, especially when the situation is certain for doom. We are living in a period that has uncertainties written all over it, but there are some who do not recognize their circumstances. For every person who says it going to get better, they have to do something to make it better. For those who do nothing, it gets worse.

When bad things happen around us, what's God purpose? The Bible says, "To every thing there is a season, and a time to every purpose under the heaven" (Ecclesiastics 3:1). Paul's purpose was to edify Christ, who is the light in dark storms. Paul was absent from the crew of the ships, indicating that he was praying to God. After consulting God, Paul was assured that he an the crew that was left with him would live. Paul glorified God and told the crew that angel of God stood by him that night. Did things get better at that moments? No, but Paul stood on the word of God. AS a matter of fact, things got worse. The ship was ripped apart. The soldiers counseled to kill the prisoners, but the centurion stopped them, and they all (276 people) had to swim ashore to a barbarians' land.

Now what God's purpose before, during, and after the storm?

Paul, before the storm, testified before King Agrippa of his conversion. Paul during the storm, testified of God's saving grace. And after the storm, Paul ministered to the sick, prayed, and laid hands to heal those with diseases. Paul fulfilled the "Great Commission" by teaching, baptizing, and observing all things as Jesus instructed us to do. Opportunity is a favorable occasion to present Christ at any time, to anybody, and anywhere. Paul used his time very wisely whether the conditions were favorable or not. The opportunity to witness for Christ was his top priority. Paul viewed his opportunity as an honor and privilege. This could only be achieved through love in which Paul received from the Lord Jesus Christ. What's God's purpose in your storms? Paul did the essentials:

- He prayed
- He listened for the voice of God
- He believed.
- He testified of what God said.
- He was delivered.
- He ministered to others.

As a result of Paul consulting God, others were encouraged and motivated to fight for their lives. When God blesses us to live to see another day, many benefits come with it. God's mercy is new, His grace is new and **his** anointing is fresh and new so that we can be fully prepared to seize the moment for Him. Paul witnessing for the Lord paid off in great dividends. Every person that survived was a witness of how God rescued them out of the storm. How can you not tell someone of what God has done for you? I'm pretty sure that every person told someone, and the good news has been passed on from generation to generation.

God is all wise and all knowing. He allows some bad to happen to prevent future harm. God has always used bad things to prevent future harm. God has always used bad things to prevent us from losing our sight. Society has depended on numerous principalities, deities, an governments that have failed and proven to be limited to fulfilling the needs of humanity. God has never failed in supplying the needs to His people, but his people have not received all their needs because of depending on other systems. When God instructed Samuel to tell King Saul

To destroy the Amalekites, He gave specific details to kill every man, woman, child, and animal. Saul defeated the Amalek, but he took Agag the king alive and kept the animals. Because of his disobedience, God rejected him as king, Samuel told King Saul, "Behold, to obey is better than sacrifice, and to hearken than the fat of rams. For rebellion is as the sin of witchcraft, and stubbornness is as iniquity and idolatry; because thou have rejected the word of the Lord, he has also rejected you from being king" (1 Samuel 15:22). Saul had the opportunity of obey God, and perhaps he would have been the great king that God had intended him to be. This illustrates to us that disobeying God only leas to bad things. Saul made it to heaven, but he cut his time short, and David became the anointed king of Israel. God give us all opportunities every day, obeying Him only leads to prosperity. When bad things happen to Christians, it is an opportunity to allow God to do several things:

- Produce godly trust - increasing faith
- Think like Jesus
- Enlighten - exposing darkness
- Continue in His wisdom- becoming wiser
- Prevention of slothfulness- steadfast
- Prosperity- soul prospering produces good health
- Inner- victory before the manifestation (seeing it before it's a reality)

You may ask, "How often will God gives us the opportunity to take the bad and make it into something good? Jesus said, "There are yet four months, and then cometh harvest? Behold, I say unto you, Lift your eyes, and look on the fields; for they are white already to harvest" (John 4:35)

STOP THINKING IN BONDAGE

Procrastinating

One of the most devastating hindrances to Christian growth is thinking negatively about what one can do and cannot do and never doing anything. In this present time, we are bombarded with advice of what to do and not to do . We are advised what to wear, how to wear it, and when to wear it. We are advised how to invest our time, our talents, and our treasures. We are advised to how to survive a recession, job loss, and family tragedy. We are advised on which medicine to take and not to take, how to be successful, where to look and not to look, and when to go ... you get the idea. This kind of thinking will limit the believer's progress and cause a dependency on things of the world rather than God. If you are living to survive, then you are not living! We must remember that Jesus said, "I come to give you life and give it more abundantly" (John 10:10).

We all have needs, but Jesus taught that we should not let materials needs disturb our trust in God. To build our faith, as God always does, the Lord illustrates this point in Matthew 6:26-34. He talked about the birds that do not store any food into barns but are fed by the heavenly Father. The grass is clothed by God and faces tomorrow without any thought. Jesus asked a question: "Are ye not much better than they?" If God takes care of the creatures and herbs of the earth and they continue to live without worrying about tomorrow, shouldn't we? Our faith in God Should be strong enough to live day-by-day, believing that whatever happens, God has already made provision for our success.

Christians are under attack every day by Satan and demons. We should understand that each day is a battle, a battle that must be won in the mind first. If you go into a battle not believing you are going to win, you probably won't. Thinking in bondage will lead you into bondage. Remember Jesus said, "So as a man think, so is he." Our faith is now being tested in every aspect concerning the Bible. The victory is not in men but in Jesus Christ. "For whatsoever is born of God overcome the world: and this is the victory that overcomes the world, even our faith" (1 John 5:4)

Little Faith

Thinking in bondage is related to little faith. When Jesus said take no thought saying what you will eat, drink, and be clothed, he was telling the believer that all their needs have been provided for. The heavenly Father knows that you have needed of these things (Matthew 6:31). In this millennium, wickedness in high places if firing darts in every possible way at humanity. Those who place their faith in the system of this world are going to be in for a rude awakening. This is why Jesus does not want the Christian to be so dependent on what we see. A prime example is when Peter saw Jesus waling on water and asked to come to him. Jesus told him to come, and Peter began to walk on water also, but when he saw the wind being boisterous, the Bible Said he was afraid and began to sink. He cried to the Lord, saying, "Save me." Jesus immediately stretched his hand to Peter and caught him and said, "O thou of little faith, why did thou doubt?" (Matthew 14:29-31). Peter's faith diminished because of what he saw. God does not work accordingly to the system of this world that He created. Peter's thinking was in bondage because of what he saw. What he saw caused him to have fear. If he had kept his eyes on the Lord, his faith would have never diminished. Little faith will produce fear and doubt. To stop thinking in bondage, commitment to positive thinking is the answer.

To exercise our faith is to read God's Word and apply His Word. The proof of our trust is manifested in work. James 2:17-18 says, "Even so faith, if it's hath not works, is dead, being alone. Yea, a man may say, Thou hast faith, and I have works: show me thy faith without thy works, and I will show thee my faith by my works. " I truly believe when things go bad, it is because we allow our thoughts to dictate our work ability. What I mean is the ability to solve problems in difficult times. If your mind is bombarded with problems, confusion, anger, frustration, and pressure, you need relief. This relief can be found in Jesus and His Word. He said, "Come unto me all ye that labor and heavy laden, I will give you rest" (Matthew 11:28). When Peter relinquished his thoughts to Jesus, he began to walk on water once again. He committed himself into the Lord's hands. If we commit ourselves to the Lord, He will always be there to pull us through. Bad things will happen to Christians in several ways:

1. Suddenly without warning
2. A steady and slow process
3. Problems never confronted
4. Lack of faith or none at all
5. Disobedience
6. Lack of trust, dedication, and commitment
7. Failure to recognize Satan as an evil spiritual being

It is important to always have your mind ready to do battle; that's where the victory plan is mapped out. If you have the victory in your thinking, it will manifest in your works. Proverbs 16:3 says, "Commit thy works unto the Lord, and thy thoughts shall be established." God's Word is in demand, and He needs us to supply it to the world. The reward that God have for us are unimaginable, and we should keep that in mind. Jesus gave us a perfect plan to keep our thoughts from being in bondage. He said, "Seek ye first the kingdom of God, and his righteousness; and all these things shall be added unto you" (Matthew 6:33). Those who choose to do the opposite allow Satan to occupy their minds only to be in bondage. Most Christians seek, but their seeking is very little or limited. What has accrued?

A. Seeking is the same.

1. We do not stretch our thinking
2. Not inquiring
3. Will not study differently 2 Timothy 2:15
4. Limit processing

B. Seeking is little and limited

1. Waiting for someone else to think for us.
2. Billions of dollars are made by companies, private investors, and businesses to do the thinking for people in general. God gives us the ability to get wealth but we must have a plan and implement it with careful thought.
3. No matter how negative it seems, we continue to have faith that God's will is far greater than ours.
4. First Corinthians 2:9 says, "Eyes has not seen, nor ear heard, neither have entered into the heart of man, the thing which God hath prepared for them than love him."

C. No data or lack of information

1. All His righteousness: Knowledge is God and He is power. You cannot process without information.
2. The Christian data is the Bible. You cannot function in spiritual matter with a worldly mind. Satan is a spirit, and God has given the Christian his word to defeat Satan.
3. God said, "My people are destroyed for lack of knowledge: because thou hast rejected knowledge. I will also reject you" (Hosea 4:6)

To keep our thoughts from being in bondage, a continual or constant seeking of God's Word is the real meaning of freedom. Jesus said, "If the Son therefore shall make you free, ye shall be free indeed" (John 8:36). Each day to keep that freedom is to read, study, and apply faith to daily living. The Bible is a extraordinary book with people who were just like you and me. They stopped thinking in bondage when they totally surrendered to the words of Jesus. God's purpose is to get us to refocus on Him.

When a woman for eighteen years had a demon in her back, she received the words of Jesus that changed her thoughts. She stood up, and her back was healed. Zacharias laughed at the thought of him having a boy at an old age. He was cursed of speech because he doubted God's word. When God performed His word, Zacharias's traditional thinking was changed. When it was time to name his son John. In both instances, they stop being in bondage when they allow God to freely think for them. When bad things happen, could it be that our thoughts are confused by the world rather than God?

When you receive and believe the Word of God, you can speak from the heart of God. The more you take in the Word, the more you became what the Word says you are, and have what it is you can have. Remember, "You are a chosen generation, a royal priesthood, and holy nation, a peculiar people; that you should show forth the praise of him who has called you out of darkness into his marvelous light" (1 Peter 2:9). If God thinks very highly of you, who are you to think anything less?

ELIMINATING WEAKNESS

There are many weakness that a Christian will have to fight against. Some are victorious, while others struggle not to fall prey to its seductions, and others are consumed by its appeal. Have you ever had a weakness in your amor that hindered you, pulled at you, frustrated you, and irritated you to the point of giving up? The fight was no longer in you, and you accepted it all were willing to live with it. If you are experiencing this weakness and have succumbed to it, things won't get any better. God has not created you to be dominated by depression, bills, job, lust, obsession, traditional rites, worrying, anxiety, lack of confidence, low self-esteem, anger, bad habits, and other spiritual wickedness that has caused weakness to penetrate the Christian's spiritual armor. This is exactly why God allows some bad things to happen to the Christian. Jesus said, "Watch ye and pray, lest ye enter into temptation. The spirit truly is ready, but the flesh is weak (Mark 14:38).

I met one person who always had a frown on her face. When I got to know her, she was one of the sweetest

People you could meet. Her weakness was a frown of worrying and not truly being the person she was supposed to be. Could it be that weakness can be hidden so deep that you cannot detect it until God allows something to happen? It's good to evaluate yourself from time to time for certain weaknesses. The Apostle Paul was made weak by infirmities, reproaches, necessities, and persecution but did not sin before God. God will respond to our weakness, just as he did with Paul. "My grace is sufficient for thee: for my strength is made perfect in weakness" (2 Corinthians 12:9). When bad thing happen, God has given us a chance to deny self and ask Him for strength for our defense.

When you investigate the scripture, you will find that God will test you, Why? If we are going to be like him the flesh will be tested. Several reasons God test is in bad situation:

- Prove your love- 2 Corinthians 12:9 (Most gladly)
- Honoring God - v. 10 (Take pleasure)
- Sacrifice- v. 10c (suffer as Christ)
- Fellowship- v. 10c (Getting to Know Christ)
- Total dependency- v.10c (when weak, strong in the Lord)
- Commitment- v. 11a (a fool in glorifying Christ)
- Promotion- v. 11b (exalted in due season)

Paul provided his love for the Lord by willing accepting his weakness. He quickly rejoices to know that the power of Christ would rest upon him (2 Corinthians 12:9b). Whenever the power of God rest upon you, that means His anointing continues to flow in you. Every Christian's goal is to obtain holiness. When Jesus said, "My strength is made perfect in weakness," this causes a spiritual transformation of enlightenment. Once you have proven yourself to God, he will promote you.

Now ask yourself this question: What eliminates weakness? The power of God! To get this power, we must always go to the source, which is in Jesus. Weakness can cause you to lose your soul into eternal domination. The numbers are staggering of people who loved God but were weak in the flesh. Judas, Solomon, the rich young ruler, David, Peter, and many others loved the Lord but were weak in bad situations. You have to go to the source to eliminate your weakness. Jesus said these words: "As thou hast given him power over all flesh, that he should give eternal life to as many as thou hast given him. And this is life eternal, that they might know thee the only true God, and Jesus Christ, whom thou has sent" (John 17:2, 3).

How can you eliminate your weakness?

1. Recognize your weakness (Sin of commission —act of doing and omission—what you failed to do).- Romans 3:23, 24
2. Confess it to God - Romans 8:8: "So they that are in the flesh cannot plead God."
3. Pray for deliverance- Psalm 23; Philippians 4:6, 7
4. Avoid the weakness by denying self - Galatians 5:24: "And they that are Christ's have crucified the flesh with the affection and lusts."
5. Ask God to control your thoughts. Think life like a winner. Meditate on a victorious life. (A worried husband was weakening when his wife had a child that was not his, but through a dream while meditating, God gave a revelation.) - Matthew 1:20: " But while he thought on these things, behold, the angel of the Lord appeared unto him in a dream, saying, Joseph, thou son of David, fear not to take unto thee Mary thy wife: for that which is conceived in her of the Holy Ghost."
6. Walk in victory- Philippians 4:13, 19
7. Repeat steps 1-6. The steps of a good man are ordered by the Lord: and he delights in his way. Though he falls, he shall not be utterly cast down: for the Lord uphold him with his hand (Psalm 37:23-24).

Flesh is a weakness that must be overcome by the Spirit of God. The Scriptures use the word flesh in five ways, referring to it as: (1) the body or physical being, (2) the old nature or sin nature, (3) the epidermis (skin), (4) man's immaterial nature, and (5) the whole being of man. Flesh itself is not evil, but is used to represent humanity's evil nature. This cannot please God. Christians should glorify God in their physical bodies as well as in their spirits, since both belong to God (1 Corinthians 6:20). When bad things happen, make sure the weaknesses of the flesh are eliminated.

YOU ARE NOT A FAILURE IN DOING GOD'S WILL

It is known fact that people feel they are failures when bad things happen. Success is not based on the accumulation of wealth, but how you handle failure. God makes it clear that He wants us to prosper in the right way. When we submit to God's guidance, provision, and protection, His promises are fulfilled in us no matter what the circumstances are. The Apostle Paul may have felt like a failure through trials and tribulations, but he did not stop because "greater is God in us that he (Satan) that's in the world (I John 4:4)."

How did Paul get to this point? What made him determine that though the bad calamities he was not a failure? One reason for his determination is because he simply believed whatever God said. He never doubted that he was not a failure because we was called by God not only to start a mission, but also to complete the mission. By the standard of this world, he could well be considered a failure. He lost his seat in the Sanhedrin Court, was out cast from

The priesthood, and was regularly beaten. Not one would want that kind of life. It looked very demanding, but Paul knew Christ on a personal level.

To know the Lord is to know your reason for existing, your purpose, which allows you to know and see beyond the bad circumstances. This helps out tremendously. To know God is like knowing how to read a compass. When you start a mission, you know the direction, in which to go. If you don't know how to read a compass, you will be lost. Satan will always make things seem to be right, but the direction will be of destruction. Failure is not how things look; failure is not trusting God no matter how things looks.

You trust your training of how to use a compass with the right coordinates. No matter what you encounter, you trust that the compass works right to get you to the right location. When tested by Satan, you have to endure the spiritual battles that he will rage against you. You must have a strong faith in order to face the difficulties that Satan will place before you. This is why Paul said, **"He that begun** a good work in you will perform it until the day of Jesus (Philippians 1:1-6). God has given us a road map to follow: the Bible. If we don't read and study it, what looks bad will be bad. But if you read it and follow it, what looks bad is not when you have your compass (Bible).

Paul wrote the Philippians' epistle because of four mains reason: (1) He sought to allay their fears for him by informing them of his prison conditions; (2) he sent Epaphroditus home because of his illness that almost killed him, which caused the church to worry; (3) he urged the church to live in Christian harmony; and (4) he cautioned them about their enemies. It would seem as if Paul had failed because he was in prison; instead, he thanks the church for their gifts and for a member of the church that helped him. This church member, while ministering to Paul, got sick to the point of death. The church was distressed of the news, which caused Paul to worry about them. How to solve these problems that has a failure written all over them?

In Philippians 1:6, Paul says five things that will help the Christians not to accept what looks like failure. First, Paul used the word confident, but he says, "Being confident." To overcome what looks life failure, you have to continue in the Lord daily. Psalm 34:1 says, "I bless the Lord at all times: his praise shall continually be in my mouth. Jesus said, "If ye continue in my word, then are ye my disciples indeed; and ye shall know the truth and the truth will set you free" (John 8:31-32). He also said, "As the Father had loved me, so have I loved you: continue ye in my love" (John 15:9).

Being confident is an inward process that is fueled by the Word and ignited by the Spirit of God. To move, and have our being, our confidence is in the Lord.

Secondly, Paul said we [being] confident of this "very thing." What very thing is Paul talking about? The work of grace that God began in you! All of us were made for ministry; therefore we all have purpose. You will find

this truth in Genesis 1:27-28. We were created for God's glory, and we were commanded to purpose. God gave us a commandment to be fruitful, multiply, subdue, and have dominion in the earth. When Paul wrote the epistle to the Philippians, he was in prison on his third missionary journey. Being well connected to God, soldiers, bars, and walls could not steal his joy, because he was focused on the purpose. Paul believed that weather situation he was in, good or bad, God would provide. He knew his worth.

The third thing Paul address is a "good work" in you. We must remember that failure is to stop trying, and surrender to appease the enemy. The Christians are instructed to fight a good fight, so their works will not be in vain. The carnal Christians acknowledge that it is very important to be on time for their jobs and understand working over.

But whatever about our good works for God? We've been empowered to witness, do missions, help the poor, love, support the church, and continue to be like Christ. God is not pleased at all when we choose earthly things over Him and His church. We all know that a tree is known by the fruit in bears. Paul knew his purpose, and no matter what came into his life (good or bad), he used to opportunity for good work.

After feeding five thousand, Jesus went to the other side of the lake. The people were seeking Him not for the teaching of heaven, but to get their bellies filled. Jesus performed the miracle to keep His purpose. Jesus instructed us not to labor for meat of this world that perishes, but for meat that endures unto everlasting life. The people asked how they might work the works of God. Jesus said,

"This is the work of God, that ye believe on him whom he had sent (John 6:26-29). God always accepts good works according to his will. In Acts 10:34-35, Peter was summoned by God to preach to the Gentiles. Peter told the waiting assembly that God is no respecter of persons, but He does give favor to those who honor Him. Peter said, "But in every nation he that fear God, and work righteousness, is accepted with God."

Fourthly, God "will perform." Whenever we see things that are failure in the eyesight of the world, we must exercise our faith in God that He's in control. Knowing God is in control gives peace to His children. Christians must stay the course that is set before them no matter what happens. Trust in God and let Him Perform His promises and He promised to us. Paul said, "We know that all things work together for good to them that loves God, to them who are the called according to his purpose" (Romans 8:28).

The last things that Paul wrote in his verse six was, "until the day of Jesus Christ. "While waiting on Jesus's return, He will continue to supply our needs. We have a long history of the Lord continually working on behalf of all His people. Abraham continued to believe when it seemed impossible for him to have a son at an old age. Daniel looked to God in the fact of certain doom, believing God would provide in the lion's den. Moses was not fearful or distressed at the Red Sea. He did what all of us should do: seek the Lord in a critical situation. When bad things happen, God is always recharging us to keep moving even when failure and be held captive, or to keep following the Lord by picking up our cross daily. Being free means staying free from what feels, looks, and seems to be end. Nothing should change our course of action for the Lord. Look at it this way: Jesus is on His way back to unite with His saints. We should be on our way to meet Him to be reunited with Him. The Christian course of actions should be, "I am persuaded, that neither life or death, nor angles, nor principalities, nor things present, nor things to come, nor height nor depth, nor any other creature shall be able to separate us from the love of God through Christ Jesus" (Romans 8:38-39).

When Jesus was surrounded by so many failures, what **was** his attitude? Victory! Our church (Hosanna) theme for the year of 2009 was "Victory." I believe what the Bible says, and that the power of life and death is in the tongue. Not only do you have to believe, but also speak what you believe. Through Christ we have victory over sickness, depression, anxiety, finances, enemies, greed, lust, gluttony, and death. I speak life to all who feel like they are failures. You have victory in Jesus Christ.

SUFFERING

Suffering is not something that you get accustomed to. It is evident that God has a plan for those who suffer. One reason is to share the cross of Jesus Christ. To know Christ is to know his love, compassion, unselfishness, dedication, and faithfulness unto God. When you suffer for Christ, you experience how his heart felt, and how his mind continued to be that of righteousness. Suffering produces humbleness, and Christ certainly suffered on the cross and remained humble unto God. When his prosecutors showed Him no **mercy** He did the unthinkable and showed mercy on them. He said unto God, "Father, forgive them; for they know not what they do (Luke 23: 34). At the point of death, Christ showed mercy when He needed mercy. He not only believed in doing God's will, but understood the process of attaining mercy. Forgiveness is a powerful tool against captivity. What I mean is that you can be in bondage within yourself because of not willing to forgive.

Mercy,

To forgive is to be free. To suffer for Christ and be like Him gives a clearer understanding of His purpose and His purpose for us. Paul put it this way: "That Christ may dwell in your heats by faith; that ye, being rooted and grounded in love. May be able to comprehend with all saints, what is the breadth, and length, and depth, and height; And to know the love of Christ, which pass knowledge, that ye might be filled with all the fullness of God" (Ephesians 3:17-18).

God allows suffering so that a Christian's dependency will be that of God and not of earthly things.

Suffering can be divided into three essentials. One is the body in which afflictions can produce tremendous pain. The second one is the mind. People have suffered so intensively in their mental capacity that they were willing to take their lives. And thirdly is the soul, which is the spiritual part of all humanity.

Suffering in the body produces spiritual fruits. Spiritual fruits produce life. I've met people with terminal diseases who had the right to be bitter but had more life than those who have great health. Why? They never stop seeking God for answers. Through their seeking, they have become closer to God and found renewed strength, faith, and love for God. You will never see a more beautiful picture of Christ than those who are suffering in their bodies and yet remain humble. To know the price of Christ's suffering is to appreciate the cost of salvation. This is why Paul said, "For ye are bought with a price: therefore glorify God in your body, and in your spirit, which are God's" (1 Corinthians 6:20).

Suffering in the mind causes Christians to doubt themselves. This allows Satan to penetrate and do considerable damage. Stress, depression, agony, anxiety, helpless, loneliness, and confusion are just a few symptoms used by Satan to entrap the minds of Christians. This is where prayer becomes a mighty weapon. It's good that you read your Bible everyday, but prayer is the victory line.

When Jesus was in the garden of Gethsemane, He was worried about his disciples and the time of his departure. He wanted to make sure they really understood his teaching, and the works of the enemy. He prayed unto the Father for assurance that His work was complete for us. This caused Jesus to be distressed, even so that He sweated while praying. The Bible said that His sweat was as great drops of blood falling down to the ground (Luke 22:44). His mind was being attacked by the enemy at a great proportion that you and I cannot imagine. The example He showed us is how to defeat suffering in our minds: pray. This goes beyond ordinary prayer. I call it "intercession prayer for self." This is when you stand between your body, mind, and flesh, asking yourself spiritually, how would Jesus pray? He would seek the Father, get assurance, and respond with great faith, no matter what the answer may be.

After Jesus had gotten an answer from the Father, He quickly accepted God's will. The Bible records Jesus asking God to remove "this cup." The cup is a representation of partaking or receiving from and accepting what's in it.

Once Jesus prayed and got reassurance, he quickly to fulfill His mission. Immediately God supplied His need by sending an angel to strengthen Him (Luke 22:42-43). There was nothing wrong with Jesus's body, but what was on His mind caused great stress. If you notice, when Christ accepted His mission, God took the stress away and replenished Him. Have you ever wondered, if Christ would have not accepted His responsibility, what may have happened? When bad things happen to you, could it be you are refusing to drink of the cup that God has prepared for you. Jesus was not denying His mission; He wanted to delay His mission, but He realized that God's timing is the right time. God has given all of us assignments. Don't delay in accepting your assignment, because it could cause you enormous stress.

If the body and mind are suffering, that also means that the soul is suffering. This is the treasure (soul) that Satan wants. He uses the body and mind to get to the soul of men. The soul is the spiritual nature of man regarded as immortal. The soul suffers when it sins. God told Ezekiel, "Behold all souls are mine; as the soul of the father, so also the soul of the son is mine: the soul that sinneth, it shall die" (Ezekiel 18:4). When Christians willingly and knowingly sin, their souls are suffering. Those who continue this path are inconsistent with their walk (worship, serving, growing, and being fruitful) with God. If you are not suffering to gain heaven then any other suffering is in vain. Why suffer for something that's not going to benefit you? The greater the suffering for righteousness, the greater reward you will receive from God. The soul (thoughts and emotions) determines the health of the body and mind.

When the apostle John wrote his last epistle to Gaius, he hoped he received two things, (1) prosperity and (2) health. He said in his third epistle, "Beloved, I wish above all things that thou mayest prosper and be in health, even as thy soul prospers" (3 John: 2). When the soul suffers, it has a void, a thirst, and a hunger to be filled. If a Christian's soul is not in proper order with God, expect the body and mind to be out of order. To be whole can only be achieved by pouring self out to the Spirit of God. The soul comes from God. Who is better to end the suffering? When Job's soul suffered, he did what all Christians should do-that is, acknowledging God's justice. The Bible said, "He was a perfect and upright man, one that feared God and eschewed evil" (Job 1:1). He held to his integrity and would not curse God. Job did several things when his soul suffered:

1. He praised God - "Bless be the name of the Lord" (Job 1:21).
2. Communicated with God-"My soul is weary of my life; I will seek in the bitterness of my life" (Job 10:1). You may be surprised, but a lot of Christians stop communicating with God when bad things happen.
3. Reverenced God - "Let me be weighed in an even balance, that God may know mine integrity" (Job 31:6).
4. Submitted to God - "Thou can do every thing" (Job 42:2).

Suffering for Christ always produces God's favor. As God blessed the latter end of Job's life, He will do the same for all His children. Remember, God is working a far more exceeding glory than we can image, that we may attain our seats in heavenly places (Ephesians 2:6, 7). Too many Christians are suffering because their relationship with God is inconsistent, not being a worshipper but a traditionalist. Most Christians go to church because their took them and through the years continue to do so parents out of tradition. Their souls never experience a true worship experience, just a religious ritual. When the soul is in full fellowship with God, the life of a Christian is manifested in service, witnessing, and worshipping. Being a Christian is no longer something you do, it is you. Job was able to endure his suffering because his soul belonged to God. It is amazing what you can endure when your soul is in God's hands. When bad things happen, first and foremost, make sure your soul is well secured in God. If it's not, the body and mind won't prosper according to God.

WHO CAN YOU COUNT ON? WHO CAN YOU TRUST?

When bad things happen, who can you really depend on? Loved ones, friends, and other Christians are a good reliable source. But when they cannot help you, who can you count on? There's no question about it, God is the most reliable source anyone can count on. Answer this question: if you can count on someone, can you trust them? Just because you can count on someone being there for mean you can trust them to do the right thing for you. you does not

Psalm 46:1 says, "God is our refuge and strength, a very present help in trouble." You can count on God being a shelter and protection from danger and distress.

Throughout history, God has proven to be a reliable source that will not and cannot fail. Society is looking for things of this world to bring them peace, security, and happiness, but fail to understand that there is no real peace, security, and happiness without God. Some of the most familiar scriptures have been overlooked and not profoundly meditated upon by Christians. We've read and heard Jesus say, "Come unto me, all ye that labor (weary) and are heavy laden, and I will give you rest. Take my yoke (attach to) upon you, and learn from me, for I am meek (gentle) and humble in heart; and you shall find rest for your soul" (Matthew 11:28-29). Now that's a scripture you can count on, but it will not manifest until we do something.

The first thing Jesus said is "come." If you want something, you will go get it. If you are hungry, you will go get food; if you are sick, you will go to a doctor; and if you are cold, you will find a warm place. Jesus Christ said, "Come." That means to go to Him in prayer with humble submission, seeking Him with all your heart, mind, and soul. Once you find Him, you've found someone that you can always count on and trust. Attach (yoke) yourself to His wisdom, power, strength, and most importantly love. When bad things happen, could it be that you have unyoked yourself from God spiritually? When you are yoked with God, He will be a "very present help in trouble."

When bad things happen, who can you trust? You need someone who is strong, is mighty, is faithful, is compassionate, is a proven winner, loves unconditionally, wants to see you blessed, fights your battles while you rest, has been with you in good and bad times, and wants you to live a life of abundance. No one can give you those things more than Jesus, because no one else is qualified.

The word yoke has a physical terminology. It is a wooden or steel bar or frame by which two animals are coupled at the head or neck together for working. Whatever direction they go, they go together. If one animal stumbles, the other animal will brace itself to help the stumbling animal get its balance. They work together to accomplish a purpose. When we are yoked with God, we can trust Him whenever we stumble to be our strength to balance our steps.

We can trust God that when we are about to take the wrong turn, He will pull us in the right direction. Whenever we are in despair, we look at Him and find hope and deliverance because we are yoked with Him. David said, "It is better to trust in the Lord than to put confidence in man and princes" (Psalm 118:8, 9).

If someone asks God to write a character reference about you, what do you think He would write? Would it be what you expect or totally the opposite? I was reading the newspaper about a teacher who was asked by one of her former students to write a character reference for a teaching position. She wrote very nice things about her and gave her recommendation. When she was contacted by the educational committee, what she wrote turned out to be completely opposite of what they found out about her former student. She found out that her former student had a history of forging fake IDs to buy alcohol while underage, numerous episodes of binge drinking in high school and college, use of marijuana, and sexual activities on social networking sites. The teacher was shocked because it did not match the person she once knew. Her conclusion of the whole matter was that young people, however intelligent, lack integrity, character, judgment, and common sense. Who can you trust that has these attributes and more than we can imagine, the Lord Jesus Christ.

If you were asked to write a character reference for God, what would you write? He's faithful, meek, strong, giving, trustworthy, longsuffering, always in control, merciful, loving, slow to anger, forgiving, a provider, best friend, comforter, and much more. If anyone did a background check, they would add to the list His goodness and righteousness.

To be unyoked from God is to be yoked with uncertainty. When bad things happen, get unyoked from trusting mammon and man, and put your trust in God. You can count on Him in everything. There are so many things that have the world's attention: violence, natural disasters, poverty, loss of jobs and homes, loss of love ones, killing, wars, political wars, and other calamities. When God for yourself, you know that it only takes Him a moment you know to turn things around. David said, "I would have lost heart, unless I had believed that I would see the goodness of the Lord in the land of the living. Wait on the Lord; be of good courage, and he shall strengthen your heart; Wait, I say, on the Lord!" (Psalm 27:13, 14).

Don't Be Lazy

Let love be without dissimulation (hypocrisy). Abhor that which is evil; cleave to that which is good. Be kindly affectionate one to another with brotherly love; in honor preferring one another; Not slothful in business; fervent in spirit; serving the Lord; Rejoicing in hope; patient in tribulation; continuing instant in prayer; Distributing to the necessity of saints; given to hospital. Romans 12:9-13 (KJV)

We can count on God and trust Him to walk side by side with us, but He expects us to work for Him and not be lazy. If you don't fight for your salvation, expect something bad to happen. To every leader in the church, the worst leader is an ineffective leader. How does the church suffer? Leader who set down on the job? In order to get your pay, you must work. When Christians sit down on the job, that means Satan is up and at it. How many people are in bondage because of no works to keep them free of depression and oppression? When the Christian works, they are moving to an end result.

As long as we have breath, we praise the Lord by our deeds, not just clapping our hands and saying long prayers. I often remind myself of the old African proverb,

"When you pray, move your feet." Don't just ask God for His power, but use it to accomplish His will. This requires careful strategic planning with a goal to be accomplished. Once you have implemented the plan, you have to work it. you have a plan and never put it to work, you will not accomplish anything. If you never pick up your Bible and read it, it will only occupy space.

When Paul was addressing the Thessalonian church from Corinth, he was concerned of misrepresentation of the gospel. He was encouraged by their faith and steadfastness, but disturbed by their work ethics. Some believed that the day of the Lord had already come and there was no need to work for that day any longer. Because of their slothfulness, some became undisciplined, and busybodies. Paul said, "For, even when we were with you, this we commanded you, that if any would not work, neither should he eat" (2 Thessalonians 3:6). When you are lazy, you will not be able to enjoy the full goodness of God. When Christians work, the Bible says the "laborer is worthy of his reward" (1 Timothy 5:18; Matthew 10:10).

You may ask, "How important are your works?" The Bible can answer that question. In Revelation the second chapter through the third chapter, Jesus said to the seven churches, "I know your works and labor." Each church was judged by their works, and we all shall be judged of our works, good or bad (1 Corinthians 3:11-15). Can God count on us to work or count on us to show up and do nothing? We can count on people to come, but can we trust them to do anything effectively when they get there? How important is our family, jobs, and status among society? Do we care more about these things than we do about God? When bad things happen, who can you count on and trust to be there for your personal needs? The Lord Jesus Christ!

ANSWER THE CALL

When the angel told Gideon he was called by God and that God was with him, Gideon was confused. The angel also called him a "mighty man of valor" (Judges 6:12, 13), this caused Gideon to ask a question: "If the Lord is with us, why has all these things happened?" Gideon had witnessed many calamities on Israel because of their evil deeds. The Midianities and the Amalekites would come upon them and take their livestock and destroy their crops. This caused Israel to be greatly impoverished. Can you live in peace when the enemy comes and take your things on any given day and destroy what you worked so hard to obtain for and your family? This went on for a number of years. They prayed to God for deliverance, but there was no answer. God's plan was for Gideon to be His mouthpiece for righteousness. God told Gideon that He would save Israel from the hand of the enemies.

What if God called upon you for a very important task? Would you do it or have an excuse? Gideon had a good excuse; he told God his family is the weakest in the tribe of Manasseh, and he was the least in his father house (v. 15). God is looking for someone He can count on and trust to do His will. Why not you? I've got news for He's calling you to do for Him every day. Jesus said, "Go therefore and make disciples of all the nation, baptizing them in the name of the Father, and of the Son and of the Holy Spirit, teaching them to observe all things that I have command you; and lo, I am with you always, even to the end of the world" (NKJV. Matthew 28: 19-20).

Can God count on you? Can he trust you? Have people come

to you about their problems, or someone come to for advice, or a particular task someone wants you to do, but you felt like you were not qualified? God placed us in a problematic world so that we can give the right answer and right solution, which is Jesus. Remember, God said we are the salt of the earth. Gideon had some excuses, and that was good because he saw the seriousness in what God wanted him to do. We all need to do a checklist on ourselves and admit our faults to God. The reason God chose Gideon was because of honesty. God knows what we can and cannot do, so when He calls you, can he count on you and trust you to do the right thing? He told Gideon two things: (1) surely He was with Him, and (2) He would defeat the enemy (v. 15). In Judges 7, Gideon was successful because he answered the call of God. God could count on Gideon and trust him because he knew Gideon capability. God knows your capability as well. Answer His call.

CONCLUSION

Every Christian will have some bad things happen to them. Satan will be behind many of those bad things. As Christians, we must be sure that we have obeyed God and not caused tribulations to ourselves. The battle is much easier to fight when you know why and who is causing the problem. When bad things happen, learn to view them as challenges. Cicely Tyson, American actress, said, "Challenges make you discover things about yourself that you never really knew." I can attest to that!

When I was in the Gulf War, operation Desert Storm, Desert Shield, I said a lot of things that I would not do, but when it became a matter of life and death, those words quickly changed. I discovered things about myself that I did not know. God truly had to keep me sound because of the many bad things that were happening. Today I can thank Him for His guidance and strength. A lot of bad things happen for a reason. Rather it is to test our love, faith, and commitment to God or to keep us in the right direction. One thing is certain, God is at the center of everything; therefore, we know He is working a far more exceedingly plan for our good.

God is trying to mold us into that perfect vessel for His glory. We are not yet a finished product, but through every trial and tribulation, every bad thing, ever closer to perfection we get. If our faith never diminished, never falls apart, and never doubt, it's just a matter of time before the bad becomes good. Paul said, "Does not the potter have power over the clay, from the same lump to make one vessel for honor and another for dishonor?" (Romans 9:21). When bad things happen, can God use our vessel to honor Him? I believe we, as Christians, can eliminate some bad things in our lives if we accept responsibility. Whenever sin accrues, we must deal with it by repenting and asking for forgiveness. We have a responsibility to represent Christ in the best possible way that we can. When bad things happen, we must maintain our integrity by being humble unto God. Once Christ saved us, we have vows to keep by being an example no matter what happens (good or bad); we realize our worth. Always, we are looking for opportunities to conquer our enemy, Satan. We should not allow bad things to occupy our mind, which leads to bondage in thinking (procrastinating).

When bad things happen, God wants us to eliminate our weaknesses. Finding out that you have some weaknesses does not mean you are a failure. Many suffer and never find out why. What God is doing? Focusing our attention on

Him? When a Christian comes to the final analysis, it is God he can count on, and it is God that he can always trust. When bad things happen to you, what is God purpose?

www.ingramcontent.com/pod-product-compliance
Lightning Source LLC
Chambersburg PA
CBHW051241120626
46547CB00014B/1743